memories
of summers
in brist
near gradac
and
other poems

memories
of summers
in brist
near gradac
and
other poems

sonja besford

Here from Elsewhere

ÆB

AB

First published in 2006 by Ambit Books,
17 Priory Gardens, London N6 5QY, UK
© 2006 by Sonja Besford
Cover image © 2006 by Vanessa Jackson
The moral rights of the author and artist are asserted in
accordance with the Copyright, Designs and Patent Act, 1988

All rights reserved. No part of this publication may be reproduced,
stored in a retrieval system, or transmitted, in any form or by any means,
electronic, mechanical, photocopying, recording or otherwise without the prior
permission in writing of the publisher.

ISBN 0-900055-08-1

A limited edition (1–25) is available in a slipcase,
signed by author, artist, designer and publisher, at £25.
Order direct from Ambit, 17 Priory Gardens, London N6 5QY, UK

Designed by John Morgan studio
Cover image by Vanessa Jackson
Printed in Great Britain by The Lavenham Press
Distributed by Central Books
The publisher acknowledges the financial assistance of Arts Council England

always to john

and for our children, class VIII2 from the primary school
oslobodioci beograda, in belgrade, wishing them farewell, god speed
and many good summers

ana bogut
mina vještica
rastko vujašković
boško gatar
nemanja grandov
stevan djordjević
ana djurović
dušan janković
jovana milovanović
marko mitranić
milica modrić
nikola pačić
tatjana petrović
milan rodić
vukašin simić
aleksandar stanojčić
tamara habaš
jovana crepulja
vanja čokorilo
fahreta džaferi

contents

PART I

memories of summers in brist near gradac *1*
ancestors *2*
gangster *3*
businessman *4*
lover: jb *5*
one love *5*
a widow *6*
cat's lament *7*
the ghost and the beauty in lagos *8*
remaining a mystery *9*
subjects in lagos *10*
an old dancer *12*
famous lover's decision *13*
erato and the future poet *14*
sunday love *15*
74. birthday *15*
before you *16*
deaf and dumb *18*
soul cleansing *19*

PART II

copy of the kama-sutra speaking *20*
mysterious word speaking *21*
the dining table speaking *22*
bedroom speaking *23*
coffin speaking *24*
tarot cards speaking *25*
an old blanket speaking *26*

PART III

subjects in the cold winter of '93 / '94 belgrade *27*
signs *29*
saluting harold pinter *30*
getting power *31*
an old nazi *32*
diplomat *33*
former warrior *33*

PART IV

eucalyptus *34*
camphire *36*
weeping willow—salix babylonica *37*
camellia, oki-no-nami *38*
willow *39*

sećanja na leta u bristu blizu gradca

dani su bili dugački, mekani i tromi
razvučeni u spore somotske sumrake
kao pohotne, mirišljave bludnice
ispružene na brokadnim jastucima divana
nogu izduženih ka obećanju prema
ne tako spokojnoj noći dok su se sveštenici
molili za vernije vernike sa veštinama
vodoinstalaterstva ili popravkom krovova,
za pastire u povratku i ribare u odlasku,
žmirkajuci da ugledaju u crno obučene udovice
kako se svlače u maslinjaku i trče nage
u nikada-trulo more da zaplivaju kao sirene
u potrazi za još jednim ljubavnim smrtnikom,
tada bi i slepa marija skrivena olijanderima
na balkonu okrenutom moru, zapevala verdija,
prestali bismo da peremo zube čekajuci njeno
visoko e, držeci ga, držeći, sve dok se noćne zavese
ne bi podigle nad svetom meseca i blistavih zvezda
da pozdrave našu mladost i tanan zahvat mudrosti

PART I

memories of summers in brist near gradac

daylights were long, soft and lazy
stretching into slow velvety dusks
like voluptuous perfumed harlots
sprawled on brocaded cushion divans
extending their limbs towards
the promise of a not so serene night while
priests were praying for truer believers
with skills to mend roofs and plumbing,
for shepherds returning and fishermen
setting out, squinting to see black-clad widows
disrobe behind the olive trees and run naked
into an undecaying sea and swim like
mermaids looking for another mortal love,
when blind maria hidden by oleanders
sang verdi on her balcony facing the sea
we stopped brushing our teeth to wait for her
high e holding holding it until the night-curtains
rose into the world of moon and starlight
to greet our youth and slender hold on wisdom

ancestors

my silence salutes heavy secrets of the dead
who withdrew from the visible world
to roam over the fine mountains and frighten
eagles and hawks into reshaping the clouds;

i sometimes wonder if, while tip-toeing
in a fog of foreign rules, i lost sight of my
ancestors' humorous games in
outwitting the quicksand of human mediocrity
which whistles to a tune named survival;

i often stroll around the roundabout of doubts
carving my affections in unforgettable words
like a master-butcher who reassembles
parts and tastes of only good loves and i say,
tonight there will be another solitary party
for my ancestors accustomed to forgiving me

gangster

he knows how to cut with a single slice
any larynx and both carotids,
how to break a tibia and fibula
or shatter a patella,
how to shoot straight through a heart,
or splatter an abdomen,
he knows how to administer morphine
against pain or for death;
so handsome, cool, remote in everything,
this damned-from-birth venom-anointed son
still shows vestigial mercy and grace
when he scatters credible promises
as subtle and layered as sahara storms
to dazzle his many women's eyes
melting their decency down
into his unblushing seduction and
thus blinded and spell-bound they dance
a triumphant waltz, leaping, whirling,
gliding just like mayflies above
the calm waters of the hungarian danube
while his starched heart watches
captivated by the beauty of each female,
each leap and whirl and glide
for they map his life-long quest
to find the womb of his own beginning
before her unchaste running scent
completely disappears
together with the memory of his tongue
wrapped in the taste of her sugar
from the milk he suckled only once

businessman

i drove slowly into destiny's spaghetti junction
(the arbiter/road-planner sat on the bonnet);
you're already mourned for, he wrote on the glass,
by hypocritical layers of ancestors, i answered immediately,
sarcastic, indifferent, cleverly business-like;
i overtook other participants, plucking their eyelashes easily;
i knitted efficient fringed traps, tamed my enemies with bribes,
entertained and married an expensive slut with a title;
my compassion was trim, my generosity diminutive;
i rarely thought, i never regretted, i never cried;
(the arbiter/road-planner sometimes applauded);
then suddenly there she was: i stopped, she entered—
isabella: who laughed with elysian lips and illegible teeth;
later, she bit: she liked unbuttoning wet skin, finding new hedonistic
points, draining the gluey overspill;
unexpectedly with her i thought frequently, regretted much,
cried often, embraced humanity, forgot eyelashes, traps, bribes,
sarcasm, indifference, business; i forgot my embedded tart;
(the arbiter/road-planner smiled, surprisingly touched);
i drove fast in a live wire with my beautiful isabella
not seeing the arbiter's/road-planner's scissors or hammer:
the brittle result of a late love on crutches—she left suddenly;
isabella vanished to belong nowhere and to no one;
i never was her real love although she was my only love;

i still drive in the spaghetti junction, in the isolated wire;
i participate, tie thoughts, celebrate, but greet nothing;
(the resigned arbiter/road-planner sleeps under the bonnet);
all around me there's a smell of snow wherever you are
isabella

cat's lament

at my very old master's glamorous funeral
there were many majestic ladies in black hats
some with veils, most in fur coats and pearls,
standing still, gloved hands, bodies shrivelled,
curled like a resurrection plant waiting for a new
rainy season to uncoil its branches and live
bravely once again;
tranquillised by sadness, vallium or dementia
each recalled, i guessed, a love episode
with my mischievous old friend who loved
difficult books, non-adhesive women and me;
so i too remembered witnessing his journeys
through troubled books and tranquil women
who halted his fickle heart for just a while
and sparkled around like jelly-fish in moonlight
dancing a quadrille while others waited;
coiled on his lap, safe, i received his tenderness
with elegant pride and feline detachment
like a local deity accepting sacramental gifts
although he knew that i was always entirely his
and i knew that he was almost always entirely mine;

later when the procession of females departs
i too shall let my grief travel up and up until
it reaches the celestial catacombs and my master's
listening ears and awaiting presence,
for i am old too and in need of his immortality

the ghost and the beauty in lagos

as she stepped to cross the road,
a bowl of plantains and yams on her head,
then quickly back at the sound of a car
her fine neck tilting to contain
the sudden reversal of momentum,
it was the fulani grace in her
which humbled me immediately
and i leapt to blend with her odours
i remembered well from long ago
when i was loved and visible to all alive
under far away northern skies and stars
in a place of cool, fox-trot shadows
over the moist just cut grass, all smells
imprisoned by my memory, now returning
mocking my invisibility and impotence;
how i long to make her mine first
to cherish her awakening eroticism
to curtsy to her and my yearning,
but alas i know
this ghostly torture shall last many life-times
until some uncapricious god hears my lament

remaining a mystery

your kindness and sweet words glide
over icons, cantos, books, theories,
cheeks, breasts, hymens and thighs;
you are in charge when loving with
your fingers' skin, thinned from caressing
and circling lower and low to crush all
your mistresses' loneliness and despair
but always skilfully hiding yours
somewhere in the basement or in the attic
of your being, no one knows;
you cry when someone real knocks
still not unlocking the inner doors
having forgotten where you've
hidden the keys, or lent them long ago
to your dead, unforgettable mother

subjects in lagos

walking along mile end road and under the green bridge
suddenly i remembered the good year of 1973 in lagos
staying at the guest house in the middle of the hausa
goat market smelling of animals, yams fried in palm oil
and cassava stew with its heat hazing away in the distance
towards the bridge which stopped in mid-air like a timeless
warrior hovering above a ravine, daring doomed lovers;
we ate giant prawns with garlic and chilli in the lebanese
restaurant in apapa, drank cool chablis from chilled glasses
discussed kant's separate self, god's and our own immortality
and how little we knew about love and loving and yet so much;
we were amused by the stranded ships pregnant with their
waiting-to-burst swelling cargo: tonnes of cement which set
speedily in the tropical humidity—an expensive oversight
by customs officers, an act of vengeance, or an ingenious
insurance swindle, no one knew;
we swam in the pool of the federal palace hotel, sipped
pints of beer with mr. negro's unforgettable steak sandwiches;
we listened to the tales of war, hate, unforgiveness and love,
we watched fulani women move as if on a parisian cat-walk,
admired the yorubas' tall stories and the ibos' masked plays;
we danced, loved and got used to handing out "dash", laughing
that, at least on that point, it was no different from america;
we met an academic from boston whose mistress sent him
weekly parcels of pornographic books so we too read

"the happy hooker" by xaviera hollander, madame with a huge
heart, or so she said, and other more and much less chaste gems
by humorous pseudonyms whose unfunny perversions and
savage ideas sometimes made us shiver in the heat of the lagos
summer; bewildered, i listened to an adulterous wife, too blonde
and too too english who nevertheless cut her veins twice
and swallowed mogadon thrice in the hope of keeping her pretty
nigerian lover who'd read economics in england and declared
unconditional hatred for all whites;
there was bob, an english psychologist with a beautiful ghanaian
lover, who claimed that in england he had learnt about the head
but had to come to africa to learn about the heart;
i witnessed the first secretary of the american embassy, a cold-
hearted bitch, push a blind beggar down a flight of stairs for
begging at her door, and the russian ambassador offering me
the freedom of their library and cinema while the yugoslavian
equivalent pretended i didn't exist;
we travelled to dahomey and swam in ocean waves as big as
fishermen's huts and were drummed out of a village celebrating
an ancient deity who tolerated no white intruders and, we were
told, ate them a few decades before;
we were stopped by armed bandits on the dark road to ibadan,
but in that good year of 1973 we were as tranquil as angels
in paradise and half a life-time away from multiple inner fears
waiting to be born

an old dancer

an imaginary clock is making her move
in the measured step of a dancer who
jumps high with the muscles of a teenager
apple-breasts and virgin heart,
lungs pink, shaded only by secondary smoking—
there is nothing to stop her remembering
being young again, today on the platform
of sloane street underground station
in front of a safe, uninterested audience:
one future mother with a diamond in her navel,
one pickpocket in pin-striped suit,
one rumanian accordion player
all in haste to depart somewhere
all determined not to see or be seen
and so she dances and dances
until the incoming train applauds

famous lover's decision

he observes the night's struggling mortality
and the easy stirring of flies on the chandelier;
he gathers the hair-pins from the scented pillow
having forgotten who sleeps under the duvet;
another single journey across young skin
and puzzled senses: a disclaimer he invokes
ever since a green-eyed unreticent woman
somersaulted into his reality then departed
without farewell to dream herself into all his
nights and replace all the female faces he shall
ever caress but never love again

erato and the future poet

he fell asleep at once; in his dream
i showed him many freedoms: from parents,
neighbours, critics and drugs, then
conceptions of estrangement and pain,
malicious confusion of irresolute words,
sacrificial loneliness and despair;
i chained him to young and dry virgins
to curly women of lightning and fire
to hooks of the first significant verses
always female always fragrantly dangerous;
i whispered into his dreaming ear:
wake-up, now you belong entirely to me,
i am sharp-tongued and unpredictable
always conditionally gentle and forgiving

sunday love

in the darkness of one plain sunday
with melted chocolate on my stomach
he drew a diagram:
the crossroads of 22 paths singing—
he didn't know who i am,
four worlds or a pentagram in the third eye;
we ate mango in the bath and something else
we drank cognac in bed and something else
he smelled of oleander and mimosas in february
he embraced me divinely but he never asked
why and where i shall go or if and when I shall return—
i closed the door quietly thinking of the infinite knot

74. birthday

fur on smooth skin. cared for. very.
only under a magnifying glass glimmer scars.
lover is from india. young. industrious.
gentle. decisive. now sleeps. dreams.
last night he read her the mahabharata. badly.
after, he grew silent. wise. brilliant.
champagne was cool. cool.

before you

in all the time before you
there was so little to recognise
in my reality among realities
or in the near moon and far stars
ascending and descending
mocking a coquettish destiny
i have never been able to ignore:
travel, don't stop travelling
even if it is under a feather duvet,
keep travelling!
in all the time before you
life was a muddle of dimmed light
with stumbling human shadows
and walk-on comedians who cloyed
through my perplexities and questions
then promptly regurgitated my essence
with the nonchalance of hunters
who shoot a mother-wolf
because in the savage winters
in that forsaken land of mine
she might be hungry enough to raid a village,

for a lamb, or even, they say, a human baby;
just before you
during one moonful midnight
my sadness eclipsed even the celestial
indifferences, perhaps because belgrade
slept snoring, as if ready, as if hovering,
glowing above the exit to its own purgatory,
disinherited from its spiteful history,
its evil relics and there was peace
oh, such blessed by gods peace
with the scent of linden trees
lilac and love at the first entrance—
suddenly, i remember well,
exquisite as that luminous darkness,
a large bird winged above my head,
shshshshshshsh,
her down-draught breezed through my hair,
her beak almost touched my scalp,
her shit landed on my forehead
and i knew then
soon you shall find me

deaf and dumb

he is a lone child in the hills above florence
a patron to maggots, spiders and ants
every year conducting southern winds to greet
returning ducks, storks and painted ladies,
later to play hide and seek with vines and olive trees
and in defending threatened cherries and tomatoes
he feels the tremor of ringing peals and thunders
always on the inner side of an impatient silence
as if waiting for a sudden rain which would
glaze his chalked life and teach him to know why
above all he yearns to laugh until tears come
and his stomach hurts, just as, it seems, others do

soul cleansing

with the hazel cane
turn the mamba three times
boil it in goat's milk
say amen nine times
strip the snake's skin
set it on fire
inhale the smoke deeply
exhale it towards the sun
see the spasm of your demons
in agony in the flaring light
start walking slowly, slowly,
do not run, do not turn
they are still following you
now like feathers, soft, black
freckles against the clouds

PART II

copy of the kama-sutra speaking

in a moody room of coasting pleasures
i live in an ancient chest with glass drawers
seeing myself in a mirror with younger
than mine memories of untroubled passions,
true loves or invasions with no mercy;
i have been caressed by matriarchs
in their rebellion against unloving husbands
but needing to please their secret lovers
who marvelled at the fusion of their unexpected
love mastery with leftovers of real chastity;
i have been leafed through and skip-studied
by drug-dealers and pimps who fingered rosaries
while injecting heroin into the veins of tired tarts;
i have been adored by the foul and the beautiful,
ignored by imbeciles, luminaries and academics
and now with silverfish and booklice as companions
each day I am less complete and more mysterious

mysterious word speaking

do you love me so richly,
so like a bone with a double marrow,
that you believe you know me?
do i please you so much
that my post-coital confessions
seem more than squintings at truths
more sideways than you can imagine?
those layers of historical shit
slid over my contours
with the speed of foul rumours
invented by scores of the unremembered—
long ago in my very first language
even when i stood quite naked,
just born and as yet unadorned,
holding my breath waiting to be dressed,
some said:
look at her sway like a troublesome beauty
dancing to enter a crystal home
and don't we desire her virginal power?
and so it began: the rape after rape,
the centuries of twisting and distorting me,
rarely graciously, except when being
the favoured concubine of love-sick poets,
who all thought they possessed me entirely
while i waited and waited,
slow centuries passed and
now suddenly i have the unexpected hope
that you will undress me slowly
and discover me uncorrupted again

the dining table speaking

in his need for atonement and forgiveness
when we were alone greeting noisy dawns
it was the pretty monk who assaulted me most
disrobing and lying across my smoothness
his right hand holding a long-tongued leather whip
he flagellated his milky flesh and me!
unlike him, i could not cry, bleed, pray, confess,
i could do nothing but accept his rite and rights,
his sacraments and my mute agony
as i received scars and swallowed his blood;
had i heard his pain, had i seen the shadows
of ill omen swaying above us? no. no.
like any young fool i cursed his barbarity
his lack of decorum (he never apologised)
his love of sacrificial spectacles as if he knew
that god enjoyed and demanded this monk's theatre;
i never knew, i swear if anyone can hear me,
that he would put a chair on top of me,
rope around the iron chandelier and his neck,
then kick to hang on the dancing cord
like an unaddressed prayer in a sorting office
with no one to receive it and no one to open it

bedroom speaking

when they first moved in and opened
my door to enter me
assuming that i was blind and deaf
in other words, dead,
they made love on the parquet floor
spreading their warmth to occupy my entirety
and for some years after that
after they filled me with a bed, mirrors,
paintings and sentimental knick-knacks
i remained a space for their clotted love,
a guardian of confessed secrets,
travels through life's intrigues and fears;

then something invisible and malicious
infected their faith in each other and in me,
to hiss inside them at first sweetly, deceiving
them that all this advancing hate was temporary,
a passing danger easily set aside but soon
i could no longer protect or soothe them—
i became a keeper of their tears and tantrums,
their humourless accusations and regrets
and slowly the wall-paper lining me,
holding all their thornless love,
started to unglue and roll away from me
stripping me of memories, crippling me, so that
i remember less and less, doubt more and more:
were they really such unique and beautiful lovers
or did my unravelling jealousy invent them?
for if they were real then, how could these two
now unforgiving, resentful, spiteful, ugly people,
forget it, when i almost haven't?

coffin speaking
for Denise Palmer

it was the rain maker, satin-dressed as the bride
she would never be, or so they all believed,
with roses in her hair, never to live again,
or so they all believed, lying inside me,
who suddenly sat-up and shrieked
in the semi-darkness of the funeral home—
if i were able, i would have screamed too:
was she not supposed to have been dead
as anyone else routinely lovingly laid in us?
at first i was offended,
then i shook in anticipation of a proof
that something had continued to live
after a (formally) certified death,
(perhaps i shall be a living oak again),
when she lifted her arms to tear the roses from her head
pulling out fistfuls of her hair as well;
she chanted words unknown to me
spitting them in tongues of foaming rage
until lightning arrived and thunder trampolined off
her upturned palms—now i trembled with fear;
child-like flames pirouetted from the room corners
towards us, licking the walls, the wooden floor,
other empty or occupied coffins,
all elegant friends of mine, oh, how those flames
adored one another!
they danced, kissed and tickled each other
i swear i could hear them giggling and singing
until the rain maker rapped on my exterior,
like the dull thuds of a tropical downpour
hitting corrugated shanty-town roofs
then the ceiling above us opened and some
urgent light lifted her up and further further up,
to become a living star and nothing more

tarot cards speaking

my gypsy keeps me in a white lace scarf
on an oak table polished for two hundred years
by her family's fortune-teller hands which soothe
my major and minor arcana with trusting devotion;
those who seek us, my gypsy and i, feel and protect
like friends do on a voyage through turbulent seas;
we read those who need the truth or those who beg
wordlessly for any old basket of comforting lies;
some balance their lives like careful wire-walkers
others fly like trapeze-artists without a safety-net
while we consume their pains and pleasures
spreading them into voiced predictions
like butter on hot pieces of toast;
we see them as children then further on and on
as surprising as clowns who have operatic voices
or as gracious and quiet as french mime-artists;
we trespass over the mine-field of unspoken secrets,
learn their dreams of perfect love or grotesque desires—
my gypsy listens
my gypsy talks
my gypsy never hurts them;
although we are yellowing and fraying with age and fatigue
my knowledge is imperishable, my love for the gypsy
and her gentle finger-tips will last as long as she does

an old blanket speaking

for many sad years
i lay in a wardrobe
in almost darkness
conversing with fleas;
i did not bother you
when you were loving
someone without me;
all the time i recalled
when we were together
every night and i held
your scent, adolescent,
curious and bewitching;
now i am ash
in your garden
disappearing

PART III

subjects in the cold winter of '93 / '94 belgrade

it was the winter of looking for
coins down sofas and in wardrobes
to buy potatoes for the soup, milk
and bread perhaps, if lucky, while
pensioners scavenged rubbish containers
for potato-peel, soured milk at the
bottom of a tetra pack, stale bread;
it was the winter of releasing pet dogs
to see them join hungry packs and watch
their attacks on passers-by who carried
sticks and guns, shouted obscenities,
but at night, oh at night
in that defeated city of ditched joys
there was no sound except for the rabid
barking, round and round, on and on,
pointless like a prayer for an impossible
miracle, until a tired dawn broke
announcing old hungers and many new deaths
while undertakers sang heavenly songs

***

it was also the winter of merciless sanctions,
flying to budapest, bucharest, sofia or athens
boarding unheated buses onwards to belgrade
laden with medications, food and clothes
for family, friends and friends of friends
we drove through darkened villages
hamlets breathing with sinister silence
almost as venomous as mirrors in the house
of an aged actress who forgot all her lines
yet could see them all etched on her face;
we passed the lighted motel signs
neon invitations for ever cheaper joys
and stopped at a café in a petrol station
where unshaven unwashed men in bulging suits
sold smuggled petrol of dubious purity then rushed
to us mumbling offers to buy our foreign currency
and sell us anything we wanted, dead or alive;
we pretended not to be frightened, cool, cool
as if in a previous life we were all in al capone's
inner circle and were used to "pals" packing guns,
cool, cool about murdering and smuggling—
you can't harm me, we're such old mates, our
body language tried to signal as we trotted
across the tarmac in rhythm with the beat
of our terrified hearts;
unaware of the unstitched hem on her uniform
the waitress hobbled on her tired, flowering heels
to serve us tea with red hands which through
the years must have launched thousands of dirty
cups into soapy water,
exhaustion and illness stood still in her eyes
doubly locked by her unsmiling lips and we
hurried back to the sanctuary of our cold bus,
someone started to cry, someone else said,
may dear god help us all, and another voice
shouted, he left us long ago, and
still another above all others, fuck it all, let's sing!

signs

in search of a miraculous cure for madness,
spreading carcinoma or any other jubilant disease,
on their way to medjugorje, those single-minded pilgrims
travel from afar, seeing, listening to the murmuring
wastelands, mountains, underground rivers,
to peasants singing wolf-songs around crazy fires,
virgins dancing naked in front of oak trees
and nymphs cutting healing sticks from hazel bushes;
they even notice poppies swaying in twilight
as if waving "good hunting" to awakening bats,
all angelic signs, they believe, all messages from God
all in need of proper decoding and in danger of being
replaced instead by devious evil spirits,
who stalk and hunt all travellers in that country
famous for being their preferred dwelling,
on that land of a thousand tears above mass graves,
burnt houses, raped women and familiar fears
so old and yet always so painfully new;
isn't it strange, Mother, isn't it very strange
how hardly anyone of those with sickness fermenting
inside them like the widows' laments all around us,
strays sideways, just a little distance from the road
towards their possibly extended mortality,
to enter a place of multiple hungers
where each embrace is shared by five or more orphaned
children and each love they receive is as frail and temporary
as a blade of grass in a desert, isn't it so very strange
that they do not think to love us for the duration of a single hug

saluting harold pinter

i'm saluting the noble harold pinter because
it takes a brave and thinking man
to fly against the gusts of slaying winds
swelling across the atlantic, chilling us with
shifting, homicidal speeches and lethal threats
which promise a long future of frothing blood
over many lands—for years and decades
the mothers of the dead shall wail their curses
towards bush and blair, earthly tyrants,
evangelical thugs who like stilt-walkers
dispensing from above their murderous platitudes,
bless the swamp of the hoi polloi
with a fatamorgana of velvety lies and ardent claims
that soon we shall all be safe and happy,
silent and tolerant as any carpet in a child's nursery
whose pile is thick with acid sick and adored shit
as long as we continue to support the merchants
of death and make them richer, as long as we
go on ignoring the maiming and killing

i'm saluting harold pinter because he lights
an almost impossible hope that his words
may hinge the warmongers' unhinged compassion,
quell the dark mutiny of their minds and senses
and make us believe again in who and what
our leaders could be, if only we could catch
their reckless ambitions and imprison them forever

getting power

you moisten with dry wine naked ambition,
her thighs, stomach, nipples, breasts;
you sit on her tongue: she squirts thick oil;
slip and fall: incautious, affectionate, trusting,
they break their arms, legs, ribs;
outcome: the losers' public castration;
you cull them below her dark gaping navel

an old nazi

in the park hotel near the salamis ruins and famagusta
i met an old austrian nazi with a gestapo past
in serbia all those decades ago—
he was shameless, icy and detached,
like the innocent and priestly guardian of some
stranger's horrible confessions
and not the memories of his own crimes—
i trembled at recalling stories told
by my surviving relatives and their friends but
he expressed no guilt and no apology while
i was gripped by the unspeakable possibility
that he may have tortured my uncle my aunt
killed one first cousin and crippled another—
no god or goddess from the salamis temples
no tales of earthquakes, tidal waves, sunsets,
templars, ancient heroes, villains and pirates
could calm me or anoint me and still i watched
him daily sipping cool turkish wines, eating meze
calm calm under the troubled cyprus skies
at peace at peace he sketched the waves, sandy
beach, salamis theatre, othello tower, christian
churches now mosques or sheep and goat pens
and people, always people, everyone he drew
everyone except me

diplomat

mesmerised by a little-deserving self,
his eyes dart left, right, never straight
meeting a companion's gaze—
like a passably charming scoundrel
his arrogance greets
his infantile stubbornness
almost with affection

former warrior

you emerge from behind
the maniacs' coat of arms
with a significant deficit:
one arm, one lung
fistula in the lower stomach;
ideals frozen
in a metastasis of screams;
actually, you never were

PART IV

eucalyptus

that morning i felt the weeping presence
of an old voodoo priestess who usually spoke to me
in polite tongues asking permission to gather
my bark and leaves for healing oils—
now she embraced my trunk and cried about
forthcoming winter rains and the ravenous earth
then chanted about born-again voices from the dark
who warned her of a morgue in waiting—
i understood nothing, not even when later from
the man-made garbage embankment behind me
a swarm of parasitic wasps started an over-hasty flight,
or when lazy serpents suddenly took off in the midday sun,
or the children continued dancing in spite of it;
i understood nothing, not even when at night beneath
the roar of winds and rain i felt the earth crack, shift
and moan like a woman giving painful birth to a large
child with a thinning ambition to survive—
at dawn, as the imam sang another elaborate deceit,

a landslide covered me, the circumcision tent
and all the shacks on the muddy plateau below—
my roots held to the deep rocks underneath, my branches
bent under the weight of thousands of severed clitorises,
labia majora and labia minora tumbling over aborted foetuses,
extracted, decayed teeth, chicken and babies' bones,
magic stones and talismans;
my senses were numbed and buried—maybe i died
until i heard the wailing of the old voodoo healer inviting
the vultures to gorge on this glad and unexpected feast —
the coffin-makers hammered away to the almost
inaudible tune of termites and wasps returning home
so i shook my extremities and moved my roots as if
i were a human awaking from a slow and bloody nightmare
praying that out of debris the impossible blossoms might
bloom to transcend all the foul kisses, eager knives
and the stale, moronic law

camphire

when she, the golden pharaoh's daughter,
came to solomon, his men-subjects blushed
as if surprised by some embarrassing memory:
a sexual fling with a gluttonous woman
who hooked their longing with a spicy perfume
made out of my invading and embracing oils;
we travelled, the pharaoh's daughter and i,
clasping each other's molecules, gliding over
solomon's skin until overwhelmed, they both
almost lost the will to breathe—i rescued their
senses just in time to hear all sacred animals,
scorpions, lions, hawks, falcons and cats
elegantly entering another hunting dawn—
one of many;
i was young then and in need of a fast dance with
thyme whose venus and serpents loved me too—
oh, how we skipped and jumped and settled
on skins of all shades, across continents,
ignoring wars, triumphing over the scent of death;
we still journey, my gemini friend thyme and i,
always with birds of good omen and often through
the moody dreams of the harem's ghosts sleeping
in solomon's still undiscovered catacombs

weeping willow—salix babylonica

adventurous mariners and merchants carried me from
babylon and china along tortuous caravan routes
and ships often edged by sudden, moody fogs
which obscured leaping shadows of monsters
rising up to salivate at the prospect of devouring
sailors then scattering plants, silks and herbs;
water often upheld me (and others) as if apologising
for the surely random harm her lodgers caused—
it tossed me with feminine gentleness
on to islands, mainlands and fertile soils
to be planted by curious mortals and immortals
to take root, nurtured by virgins or moon goddesses
who used parts of me for love spells, which i like,
or evil enchantments, which indeed i do not;
from the very beginning, i was adored by many
who whispered their secrets to my listening branches
while moulding their dreams and future as they sang
holding hands turned bravely to face the full moon;
through the millennia i measured one embrace
against another, perplexed by the beat of many
false hearts, but all said, assessed and weighed,
i loved no one more completely than one called
persephone, who fastened all my essences and still
alarms them with the desire to be a human hades
if only for a night

camellia, oki-no-nami
to Luigi Berliocchi

even before hypolyte charles dismounted,
the empress josephine had started dressing
and i had this craving for a crude song
to mark their frequent infidelities
and mark that inaudible pulse of longing
for each other when her tears would cause
the gentle tremors of my cousin, alba plena;
she liked the scent of camellia fraterna
but always came back to me, oki-no-nami, to me
the butterfly of enlightenment, whose purity
had guarded my masters and mistresses
(from the buddha to confucius, from the tao masters
to the jade emperor) against all sinners and all sins
which threatened them;
my petals restrained their furies
my seeds were vigilant to inherit and pass on
their prayers and dreams; i laughed with their
laughter, ached with their pain and, in the hug
of a home-bound man, when he whistled after
a passing woman in the piazza san marco,
i whistled too, albeit silently, and i remember
one luigi berliocchi,
who loved me, admired me, wrote about me
but before i could fathom his inner map
to help him design his own guardian,
he died and some sum of me died too

willow

some poets are ladies and gentlemen and scholars
some are beggars and crawlers and chisellers
some are as royal as any descendent of murderers
or as murderous as any hungry beast—
some are gold medal creeps and celestial liars
others can follow the tongues of urban foxes
into the darkness of their unkempt imagination;
i, on the other hand, live in the garden of a demented poet
with a birthday in march, who, bewildered by sudden love,
now writes verses which will, for once, at last, last
(although he doesn't know it yet);
he also doesn't know that i honour pisceans and their fast
dream-spinning conducted by neptune and venus,
and because the moon honours me with a persistent stare,
like an old spinster sitting by her window, patiently
i waited for that one twilight void of any earthly beauty
save for a woman with emerald eyes, bloodstone necklace
and lily-of-the-valley scent;
she opened the garden gates with her gloved finger-tips,
tipped them shut with her majestical bum and he shouted,
without even looking up from the curtain of my branches:
did i say, enter? did i, excuse me, say, enter?
then the mediterranean wind invaded me with male pollen,
i opened, bowing further to my own need
while my poet lifted his eyes and shivered:
come in, he said in awe, but i cared not for them
i heard nothing more, lost, lost and receiving

Sonja Batinić-Besford is one of four sisters born in Belgrade. Her three sisters still live there but Sonja came to Britain as a student and was trapped into marriage (without even being pregnant). She lives in London and visits Belgrade frequently.

Apart from her work as a playwright and critic, Sonja has published six books including: *Kako Uloviti Talasona (How to catch a Thalasson)*, a collection of short stories, published by Prosveta in 1992; *Lovci vremena (Hunters of Time)*, a novel published by Stubovi Kulture in 1997; and *Arrivals & Departures*, a book of poetry written in English and published by the Association of Serbian Writers Abroad in 2002. *memories of summers in brist near gradac* is her seventh book, and is dedicated to a class of Belgrade children of whom she and her husband have been patrons for the last eight years.

All the poems in this book have been written directly in English. The title poem has been translated into Serbian bÿ Sonja from her English version.

Some of these poems have previously appeared in Ambit, Kritika, Orbis and Wolf. The author gratefully acknowledges the editors of these publications.